HENRY

Lawson

HENRY

Lawson

A Book of Verse

ANGUS
& ROBERTSON

AN ANGUS & ROBERTSON BOOK

First published in Australia in 1990 by
Collins/Angus & Robertson Publishers Australia

Collins/Angus & Robertson Publishers Australia
Unit 4, Eden Park, 31 Waterloo Road, North Ryde
NSW 2113, Australia

William Collins Publishers Ltd
31 View Road, Glenfield, Auckland 10, New Zealand

Angus & Robertson (UK)
16 Golden Square, London W1R 4BN, United Kingdom

National Library of Australia
Cataloguing-in-Publication data:

Lawson, Henry, 1867–1922.
  Henry Lawson, a book of verse.

  ISBN 0 207 16861 X.

  I. Matthews, Brian (Brian Ernest). II. Title.

A821.2

Typeset in Century Old Style by Midland Typesetters,
Maryborough, Victoria.
Printed in Singapore

5 4 3 2 1
95 94 93 92 91 90

Contents

INTRODUCTION – *ix*

GOLDEN GULLY – *1*

THE ARMY OF THE REAR – *3*

THE WATCH ON THE KERB – *5*

FACES IN THE STREET – *6*

ANDY'S GONE WITH CATTLE – *10*

ANDY'S RETURN – *11*

THE BLUE MOUNTAINS – *13*

THE BALLAD OF THE DROVER – *14*

THE GHOST – *17*

THE ROARING DAYS – *20*

THE TEAMS – *23*

MIDDLETON'S ROUSEABOUT – *24*

THE GLASS ON THE BAR – *26*

THE PAVEMENT STONES – *27*

THE STATUE OF OUR QUEEN – *29*

DAN WASN'T THROWN FROM HIS HORSE – *30*

FREEDOM ON THE WALLABY – *31*

WHEN THE IRISH FLAG WENT BY – *32*

UP THE COUNTRY – *33*

THE CITY BUSHMAN – *36*

THE GROG-AN'-GRUMBLE STEEPLECHASE – *40*

WHEN YOUR PANTS BEGIN TO GO – *43*

THE MORNING OF NEW ZEALAND – *45*

LAKE ELIZA – *46*

OUT BACK – *47*

I'LL TELL YOU WHAT, YOU WANDERERS – *50*

REEDY RIVER – *51*

THE MEN WHO COME BEHIND – *53*

THE UNCULTURED RHYMER TO HIS CULTURED
CRITICS – *55*

THE OLD BARK SCHOOL – *56*

THE OLD JIMMY WOODSER – *58*

SECOND CLASS WAIT HERE – *60*

THE SLIPRAILS AND THE SPUR – *61*

THE RUSH TO LONDON – *63*

THE SHEARERS – *64*

THE SEPARATION – *66*

TO HANNAH – *67*

TO JIM – *68*

THE KING AND QUEEN AND I – *70*

THE HORSEMAN ON THE SKYLINE – *71*

MY FATHER-IN LAW AND I – *73*

THE GENTLEMEN OF DICKENS – *74*

DO THEY THINK THAT I DO NOT KNOW? – *76*

THE ROUTE MARCH – *79*

ON THE NIGHT TRAIN – *80*

INDEX OF TITLES – *82*

INDEX OF FIRST LINES – *84*

INTRODUCTION

W hen you read poems like "Middleton's Rouseabout" or "The Watch on the Kerb" or "On the Night Train", the argument about whether Lawson was a *real* poet or much of a poet or *any* kind of poet seems irrelevant. Lawson's poems are often rough enough: rhythms trip up now and then; there are occasionally odd or ugly rhymes (a problem worsened by his deafness); some poems ramble on without apparent structure; some of them are indeed ephemeral and second-rate. But Lawson's memorable poems have some of the strengths of his great prose. The eye for detail and human foible is unerring; the compassion for the repressed and the forgotten is as profound in "Faces in the Street" and "Second Class Wait Here" as it is in "The Drover's Wife"; the sardonic, amiably resigned wit of such stories as "The Loaded Dog" or "The Ironbark Chip" surfaces in "The Statue of Our Queen" and "When Your Pants Begin to Go"; the imaging of mateship is as powerful in the fierce "Dan Wasn't Thrown from His Horse" as it is in any of the Mitchell sketches. It's just that, in the poems, these concerns and passions and jokes find a simpler, uncomplicated, often predictable expression. This was bound to be the case given Lawson's more or less unquestioning allegiance in every poem to the so-called bush ballad form or to something not far removed from it.

Lawson worked very hard at the great stories for which he is now so justly famous but verse came with dangerous ease. His early, and in general his best, poems enshrined affectionate memory ("Golden Gully"), a growing sensitivity to social and political injustice ("Faces in the Street") and, after his trip to Bourke in 1892-93, various wry, appalled or compassionate perceptions of the outback ("Up the Country", "The City Bushman", "Out Back" . . .). More and more, though, as his personal life deteriorated, poems tended to be immediate and quickly assembled vehicles for current passions, obsessions and especially grievances. His poems became "occasional" in the worst sense of the word and that's why, in a tightly constrained selection such as this, Lawson's later work is thinly represented, even though he actually wrote a great deal of verse in the last fifteen or so years of his life.

Arguments no doubt will continue about how accomplished or how flawed was Lawson the poet, especially within "college walls", but they won't make any difference to the fact that we return again and again to so many of Lawson's poems for some of the same reasons that we return to any good and favourite writing. To hear again that honest, camp fire voice getting the tone just right, as at the end of "Dan Wasn't Thrown from His Horse"; to savour the brilliantly deft, quizzical description of Andy, Middleton's rouseabout; to listen to the drumbeat of youthful revolutionary fervour in "Faces in the Street". Or any number of other pleasant, exciting or moving reasons.

If you experience all that and more when you dip into these poems—and you will—then Lawson, as he himself might have mournfully observed, must have been getting something right.

Brian Matthews
Flinders University

Golden Gully

No one lives in Golden Gully, for its golden days are o'er,
And its clay shall never sully blucher-boots of diggers more,
For the diggers long have vanished—nought but broken shafts
    remain,
And the bush, by diggers banished, fast reclaims its own again.
Now, when dying Daylight slowly draws her fingers
    from the "Peak",
The Weird Empress Melancholy rises from the reedy creek—
In the gap above the gully, while the dismal curlews scream
Loud to welcome her as ruler of the dreary night supreme—
Takes her throne, and by her presence fills the strange,
    uncertain air
With a ghostly phosphorescence of the horrors hidden there.
None would think, by camp-fire blazy, lighting fitfully the scene,
In the seasons that are hazy, how in seasons gone between,
Diggers yarned or joined in jolly ballads of the field and foam,
Or grew sad and melancholy over songs like "Home,
    Sweet Home"—
Songs of other times, demanding sullen tears that would not start,
Every digger understanding what was in his comrade's heart.
It may seem to you a riddle how a poet's fancies roam,
But methinks I hear a fiddle softly playing "Home, Sweet Home"
'Mid the trees, while meditative diggers round the camp-fire stand.
(Those were days before Australians learned to love their
    native land.)
Now the dismal curlew screeches round the shafts when night
    winds sough;
Startling murmurs, broken speeches, shake each twisted,
    tangled bough,

And whene'er the night comes dreary, darkened by the
    falling rain,
Voices, loud and dread and eerie, come again and come again—
Come like troubled souls forbidden rest until their tales are told—
Tales of deeds of darkness hidden in the whirl of days of gold—
Come like troubled spirits telling tales of dire and dread mishaps,
Kissing, falling, rising, swelling, dying in the dismal gaps.
When the coming daylight slowly lays her fingers on the "Peak"
Then the Empress Melancholy hurries off to swamps that reek.
But the scene is never cheery, be it sunshine, be it rain,
For the Gully keeps its dreary look till darkness comes again.
As you stand beside the broken shafts, where grass is
    growing thick,
You can almost hear a spoken word, or hear a thudding pick;
And your very soul seems sinking, foetid grows the morning air,
For you cannot help believing that there's something buried there.
There's a ring amid the saplings by a travelling circus worn,
That amused the noisy diggers e'er the rising race was born;
There's a road where scrub encroaches that was once the
    main highway,
Over which two rival coaches dashed in glory twice a day;
Gone—all gone from Golden Gully, for its golden days are o'er,
And its clay shall never sully wheels of crowded coaches more.

[*Mount Victoria, December 1887*]

2

The Army of the Rear

I listened through the music and the sounds of revelry,
And all the hollow noises of that year of Jubilee;
I heard beyond the music and beyond the loyal cheer
The steady tramp of thousands that were marching in the rear.
  Tramp! tramp! tramp!
  They seem to shake the air,
Those never-ceasing footsteps of the outcasts in the rear.

I heard defiance ringing from the men of rags and dirt,
I heard wan women singing that sad "Song of the Shirt",
And o'er the sounds of menace and moaning low and drear
I heard the steady tramping of their feet along the rear.
  Tramp! tramp! tramp!
  Vibrating in the air—
They're swelling fast, those footsteps of the Army of the Rear!

I hate the wrongs I read about, I hate the wrongs I see!
The tramping of that army sounds as music unto me!
A music that is terrible, that frights the anxious ear,
Is beaten from the weary feet that tramp along the rear.
  Tramp! tramp! tramp!
  In dogged, grim despair—
They have a goal, those footsteps of the Army of the Rear!

I looked upon the nobles, with their lineage so old;
I looked upon their mansions, on their acres and their gold,
I saw their women radiant in jewelled robes appear,
And then I joined the army of the outcasts in the rear.
  Tramp! tramp! tramp!
  We'll show what Want can dare,
My brothers and my sisters of the Army of the Rear!

3

I looked upon the mass of poor, in filthy alleys pent;
And on the rich men's Edens, that are built on grinding rent;
I looked o'er London's miles of slums—I saw the horrors here,
And swore to die a soldier of the Army of the Rear.
>Tramp! tramp! tramp!
>I've sworn to do and dare,
I've sworn to die a soldier of the Army of the Rear!

"They're brutes," so say the wealthy, "and by steel must be
>dismayed"—
Be brutes among us, nobles, they are brutes that *ye* have made;
We want what God hath given us, we want our portion here,
And that is why we're marching—and we'll march beyond
>the rear!
>Tramp! tramp! tramp!
>Awake and have a care,
Ye proud and haughty spurners of the wretches in the rear.

We'll nurse our wrongs to strengthen us, our hate that it
>may grow,
For, outcast from society, society's our foe.
Beware! who grind out human flesh, for human life is dear!
There's menace in the marching of the Army of the Rear.
>Tramp! tramp! tramp!
>There's danger in despair,
There's danger in the marching of the Army of the Rear!

The wealthy care not for our wants, nor for the pangs we feel;
Our hands have clutched in vain for bread, and now they clutch
>for steel!
Come, men of rags and hunger, come! There's work for heroes
>here!

There's room still in the vanguard of the Army of the Rear!
    Tramp! tramp! tramp!
    O men of want and care!
There's glory in the vanguard of the Army of the Rear!

[January 1888]

The Watch on the Kerb

N ight-lights are falling;
    Girl of the street,
Go to your calling
    If you would eat.
Lamplight and starlight
    And moonlight superb,
Bright hope is a farlight,
    So watch on the kerb.

    Watch on the kerb,
    Watch on the kerb;
Hope is a farlight; then watch on the kerb.

Comes a man: call him—
    Gone! he is vext;
Curses befall him,
    Wait for the next!
Fair world and bright world,
    Life still is sweet—

Girl of the night-world,
    Watch on the street.

Dreary the watch is:
    Moon sinks from sight,
Gas only blotches
    Darkness with light;
Never, O never
    Let courage go down;
Keep from the river,
    O Girl of the Town!

[1888—January?]

Faces in the Street

They lie, the men who tell us for reasons of their own
    That want is here a stranger, and that misery's unknown;
For where the nearest suburb and the city proper meet
My window-sill is level with the faces in the street—
    Drifting past, drifting past,
    To the beat of weary feet—
While I sorrow for the owners of those faces in the street.

And cause I have to sorrow, in a land so young and fair,
To see upon those faces stamped the marks of Want and Care;

I look in vain for traces of the fresh and fair and sweet
In sallow, sunken faces that are drifting through the street—
    Drifting on, drifting on,
    To the scrape of restless feet;
I can sorrow for the owners of the faces in the street.

In hours before the dawning dims the starlight in the sky
The wan and weary faces first begin to trickle by,
Increasing as the moments hurry on with morning feet,
Till like a pallid river flow the faces in the street—
    Flowing in, flowing in,
    To the beat of hurried feet—
Ah! I sorrow for the owners of those faces in the street.

The human river dwindles when 'tis past the hour of eight,
Its waves go flowing faster in the fear of being late;
But slowly drag the moments, whilst beneath the dust and heat
The city grinds the owners of the faces in the street—
    Grinding body, grinding soul,
    Yielding scarce enough to eat—
O I sorrow for the owners of the faces in the street.

And then the only faces till the sun is sinking down
Are those of outside toilers and the idlers of the town,
Save here and there a face that seems a stranger in the street
Tells of the city's unemployed upon his weary beat—
    Drifting round, drifting round,
    To the tread of listless feet—
Ah! My heart aches for the owner of that sad face in the street.

And when the hours on lagging feet have slowly dragged away,
And sickly yellow gaslights rise to mock the going day,

Then flowing past my window like a tide in its retreat,
Again I see the pallid stream of faces in the street—
    Ebbing out, ebbing out,
    To the drag of tired feet,
While my heart is aching dumbly for the faces in the street.

And now all blurred and smirched with vice the day's
    sad pages end,
For while the short "large hours" towards the longer "small
    hours" trend,
With smiles that mock the wearer, and with words that
    half entreat,
Delilah pleads for custom at the corner of the street—
    Sinking down, sinking down,
    Battered wreck by tempests beat—
A dreadful, thankless trade is hers, that Woman of the Street.

But, ah! to dreader things than these our fair young city comes,
For in its heart are growing thick the filthy dens and slums,
Where human forms shall rot away in sties for swine unmeet,
And ghostly faces shall be seen unfit for any street—
    Rotting out, rotting out,
    For the lack of air and meat—
In dens of vice and horror that are hidden from the street.

I wonder would the apathy of wealthy men endure
Were all their windows level with the faces of the Poor?
Ah! Mammon's slaves, your knees shall knock, your hearts in
    terror beat,
When God demands a reason for the sorrows of the street,
    The wrong things and the bad things
    And the sad things that we meet
In the filthy lane and alley, and the cruel, heartless street.

I left the dreadful corner where the steps are never still,
And sought another window overlooking gorge and hill;
But when the night came dreary with the driving rain and sleet,
They haunted me—the shadows of those faces in the street,
    Flitting by, flitting by,
    Flitting by with noiseless feet,
And with cheeks but little paler than the real ones in the street.

Once I cried: "O God Almighty! if Thy might doth still endure,
Now show me in a vision for the wrongs of Earth a cure."
And, lo! with shops all shuttered I beheld a city's street,
And in the warning distance heard the tramp of many feet,
    Coming near, coming near,
    To a drum's dull distant beat,
And soon I saw the army that was marching down the street.

Then, like a swollen river that has broken bank and wall,
The human flood came pouring with the red flags over all,
And kindled eyes all blazing bright with revolution's heat,
And flashing swords reflecting rigid faces in the street—
    Pouring on, pouring on,
    To a drum's loud threatening beat,
And the war-hymns and the cheering of the people in the street.

And so it must be while the world goes rolling round its course,
The warning pen shall write in vain, the warning voice
   grow hoarse,
But not until a city feels Red Revolution's feet
Shall its sad people miss awhile the terrors of the street—
    The dreadful everlasting strife
    For scarcely clothes and meat
In that pent track of living death—the city's cruel street.

[*Sydney, July 1888*]

9

Andy's Gone With Cattle

O ur Andy's gone to battle now
    'Gainst Drought, the red marauder:
Our Andy's gone with cattle now
    Across the Queensland border.

He's left us in dejection now;
    Our hearts with him are roving.
It's dull on this selection now,
    Since Andy went a-droving.

Who now shall wear the cheerful face
    In times when things are slackest?
And who shall whistle round the place
    When Fortune frowns her blackest?

O who shall cheek the squatter now
    When he comes round us snarling?
His tongue is growing hotter now
    Since Andy crossed the Darling.

The gates are out of order now,
    In storms the riders rattle;
For far across the border now
    Our Andy's gone with cattle.

Poor Aunty's looking thin and white;
    And Uncle's cross with worry;
And poor old Blucher howls all night
    Since Andy left Macquarie.

O may the showers in torrents fall,
   And all the tanks run over;
And may the grass grow green and tall
   In pathways of the drover;

And may good angels send the rain
   On desert stretches sandy;
And when the summer comes again
   God grant 'twill bring us Andy.

[October 1888]

Andy's Return

With pannikins all rusty,
   And billy burnt and black,
And clothes all torn and dusty,
   That scarcely hide his back;
With sun-cracked saddle-leather,
   And knotted greenhide rein,
And face burnt brown with weather,
   Our Andy's home again!

His unkempt hair is faded
   With sleeping in the wet,
He's looking old and jaded;
   But he is hearty yet.

With eyes sunk in their sockets—
    But merry as of yore;
With big cheques in his pockets,
    Our Andy's home once more!

Old Uncle's bright and cheerful;
    He wears a smiling face;
And Aunty's never tearful
    Now Andy's round the place.
Old Blucher barks for gladness;
    He broke his rusty chain,
And leapt in joyous madness
    When Andy came again.

With tales of flood and famine
    On distant northern tracks,
And shady yarns—"baal gammon!"—
    Of dealings with the blacks,
From where the skies hang lazy
    On many a northern plain,
From regions dim and hazy
    Our Andy's home again!

His toil is nearly over;
    He'll soon enjoy his gains.
Not long he'll be a drover,
    And cross the lonely plains.
We'll happy be for ever
    When he'll no longer roam,
But by some deep, cool river
    Will make us all a home.

[*Sydney, November 1888*]

The Blue Mountains

Above the ashes straight and tall,
   Through ferns with moisture dripping,
I climb beneath the sandstone wall,
   My feet on mosses slipping.

Like ramparts round the valley's edge
   The tinted cliffs are standing,
With many a broken wall and ledge,
   And many a rocky landing.

And round about their rugged feet
   Deep ferny dells are hidden
In shadowed depths, whence dust and heat
   Are banished and forbidden.

The stream that, crooning to itself,
   Comes down a tireless rover,
Flows calmly to the rocky shelf,
   And there leaps bravely over.

Now pouring down, now lost in spray
   When mountain breezes sally,
The water strikes the rock midway,
   And leaps into the valley.

Now in the west the colours change,
   The blue with crimson blending;
Behind the far Dividing Range,
   The sun is fast descending.

And mellowed day comes o'er the place,
   And softens ragged edges;
The rising moon's great placid face
   Looks gravely o'er the ledges.

[Sydney, December 1888]

The Ballad of the Drover

A cross the stony ridges,
   Across the rolling plain,
Young Harry Dale, the drover,
   Comes riding home again.
And well his stock-horse bears him,
   And light of heart is he,
And stoutly his old pack-horse
   Is trotting by his knee.

Up Queensland way with cattle
   He travelled regions vast;
And many months have vanished
   Since home-folk saw him last.
He hums a song of someone
   He hopes to marry soon;
And hobble-chains and camp-ware
   Keep jingling to the tune.

14

Beyond the hazy dado
   Against the lower skies
And yon blue line of ranges
   The homestead station lies.
And thitherward the drover
   Jogs through the lazy noon,
While hobble-chains and camp-ware
   Are jingling to a tune.

An hour has filled the heavens
   With storm-clouds inky black;
At times the lightning trickles
   Around the drover's track;
But Harry pushes onward,
   His horses' strength he tries,
In hope to reach the river
   Before the flood shall rise.

The thunder from above him
   Goes rolling o'er the plain;
And down on thirsty pastures
   In torrents falls the rain.
And every creek and gully
   Sends forth its little flood,
Till the river runs a banker,
   All stained with yellow mud.

Now Harry speaks to Rover,
   The best dog on the plains,
And to his hardy horses,
   And strokes their shaggy manes:
"We've breasted bigger rivers
   When floods were at their height,

Nor shall this gutter stop us
　From getting home to-night!"

The thunder growls a warning,
　The ghastly lightnings gleam,
As the drover turns his horses
　To swim the fatal stream.
But O the flood runs stronger
　Than e'er it ran before;
The saddle-horse is failing,
　And only half-way o'er!

When flashes next the lightning,
　The flood's grey breast is blank,
And a cattle dog and pack-horse
　Are struggling up the bank.
But in the lonely homestead
　The girl shall wait in vain—
He'll never pass the stations
　In charge of stock again.

The faithful dog a moment
　Sits panting on the bank,
And then swims through the current
　To where his master sank.
And round and round in circles
　He fights with failing strength,
Till, borne down by the waters,
　The old dog sinks at length.

Across the flooded lowland
　And slopes of sodden loam
The pack-horse struggles onward,

To take dumb tidings home.
And mud-stained, wet, and weary,
   Through ranges dark goes he;
While hobble-chains and tinware
   Are sounding eerily.

The floods are in the ocean,
   The creeks are clear again,
And now a verdant carpet
   Is stretched across the plain.
But bleaching on the desert
   Or in the river reeds
The bones lie of the bravest
   That wide Australia breeds.

[*Sydney, February 1889*]

The Ghost

D own the street as I was drifting with the city's human tide,
Came a ghost, and for a moment walked in silence
   by my side—
Now my heart was hard and bitter, and a bitter spirit he,
So I felt no great aversion to his ghostly company.
Said the Shade: "At finer feelings let your lip in scorn be curled,
'Self and Pelf', my friend, has ever been the motto for the world."

17

And he said: "If you'd be happy, you must clip your fancy's wings,
Stretch your conscience at the edges to the size of earthly things;
Never fight another's battle, for a friend can never know
When he'll gladly fly for succour to the bosom of the foe.
At the power of truth and friendship let your lip in scorn
    be curled—
'Self and Pelf', my friend, remember, is the motto of the world.

"Where Society is mighty, always truckle to her rule;
Never send an 'i' undotted to the teacher of a school;
Only fight a wrong or falsehood when the crowd is at your back,
And, till Charity repay you, shut the purse, and let her pack;
At the fools who would do other let your lip in scorn be curled,
'Self and Pelf', my friend, remember, that's the motto of the world.

"Ne'er assail the shaky ladders Fame has from her niches hung,
Lest unfriendly heels above you grind your fingers from the rung;
Or the fools who idle under, envious of your fair renown,
Heedless of the pain you suffer, do their worst to shake you down.
At the praise of men, or censure, let your lip in scorn be curled,
'Self and Pelf', my friend, remember, is the motto of the world.

"Flowing founts of inspiration leave their sources parched
    and dry,
Scalding tears of indignation sear the hearts that beat too high;
Chilly waters thrown upon it drown the fire that's in the bard;
And the banter of the critic hurts his heart till it grows hard.
At the fame your muse may offer let your lip in scorn be curled,
'Self and Pelf', my friend, remember, that's the motto of the world.

"Shun the fields of love, where lightly, to a low and mocking tune,
Strong and useful lives are ruined, and the broken hearts are
    strewn.

Not a farthing is the value of the honest love you hold;
Call it lust, and make it serve you! Set your heart on nought
      but gold.
At the bliss of purer passions let your lip in scorn be curled—
'Self and Pelf', my friend, shall ever be the motto of the world.''

Then he ceased and looked intently in my face, and nearer drew;
But a sudden deep repugnance to his presence thrilled me through;
Then I saw his face was cruel, by the look that o'er it stole,
Then I felt his breath was poison, by the shuddering of my soul,
Then I guessed his purpose evil, by his lip in sneering curled,
And I knew he slandered mankind, by my knowledge of the world.

But he vanished as a purer brighter presence gained my side—
"Heed him not! there's truth and friendship in this wondrous
      world,'' she cried,
"And of those who cleave to virtue in their climbing for renown,
Only they who faint or falter from the height are shaken down.
At a cynic's baneful teaching let your lip in scorn be curled!
'Brotherhood and Love and Honour!' is the motto for the world.''

[*Sydney, 18th July 1889*]

19

The Roaring Days

T he night too quickly passes
   And we are growing old,
So let us fill our glasses
   And toast the Days of Gold;
When finds of wondrous treasure
   Set all the South ablaze,
And you and I were faithful mates
   All through the roaring days!

Then stately ships came sailing
   From every harbour's mouth,
And sought the land of promise
   That beaconed in the South;
Then southward streamed their streamers
   And swelled their canvas full
To speed the wildest dreamers
   E'er borne in vessel's hull.

Their shining Eldorado,
   Beneath the southern skies,
Was day and night for ever
   Before their eager eyes.
The brooding bush, awakened,
   Was stirred in wild unrest,
And all the year a human stream
   Went pouring to the West.

The rough bush roads re-echoed
   The bar-room's noisy din,
When troops of stalwart horsemen
   Dismounted at the inn.

And oft the hearty greetings
　　And hearty clasp of hands
Would tell of sudden meetings
　　Of friends from other lands.

And when the cheery camp-fire
　　Explored the bush with gleams,
The camping-grounds were crowded
　　With caravans of teams;
Then home the jests were driven,
　　And good old songs were sung,
And choruses were given
　　The strength of heart and lung.

Oft when the camps were dreaming,
　　And fires began to pale,
Through rugged ranges gleaming
　　Swept on the Royal Mail.
Behind six foaming horses,
　　And lit by flashing lamps,
Old Cobb and Co. in royal state,
　　Went dashing past the camps.

O who would paint a goldfield,
　　And paint the picture right,
As we have often seen it
　　In early morning's light;
The yellow mounds of mullock
　　With spots of red and white,
The scattered quartz that glistened
　　Like diamonds in light;

The azure line of ridges,
　　The bush of darkest green,

21

The little homes of calico
    That dotted all the scene.
The flat straw hats with ribands
    That old engravings show:
The dress that still reminds us
    Of sailors, long ago.

I hear the fall of timber
    From distant flats and fells,
The pealing of the anvils
    As clear as little bells,
The rattle of the cradle,
    The clack of windlass-boles,
The flutter of the crimson flags
    Above the golden holes.

Ah, then their hearts were bolder,
    And if Dame Fortune frowned
Their swags they'd lightly shoulder
    And tramp to other ground.
O they were lion-hearted
    Who gave our country birth:
O they were of the stoutest sons
    From all the lands on earth.

But golden days are vanished,
    And altered is the scene;
The diggings are deserted,
    The camping-grounds are green;
The flaunting flag of progress
    Is in the West unfurled,
The mighty Bush with iron rails
    Is tethered to the world.

                                    [1889?]

22

The Teams

A cloud of dust on the long white road,
   And the teams go creeping on
Inch by inch with the weary load;
And by the power of the green-hide goad
   The distant goal is won.

With eyes half-shut to the blinding dust,
   And necks to the yokes bent low,
The beasts are pulling as bullocks must;
And the shining tires might almost rust
   While the spokes are turning slow.

With face half-hid 'neath a broad-brimmed hat
   That shades from the heat's white waves,
And shouldered whip with its green-hide plait,
The driver plods with a gait like that
   Of his weary, patient slaves.

He wipes his brow, for the day is hot,
   And spits to the left with spite;
He shouts at Bally, and flicks at Scot,
And raises dust from the back of Spot,
   And spits to the dusty right.

He'll sometimes pause as a thing of form
   In front of a settler's door,
And ask for a drink, and remark, "It's warm,"
Or say, "There's signs of a thunderstorm;"
   But he seldom utters more.

The rains are heavy on roads like these;
    And, fronting his lonely home,
For days together the settler sees
The waggons bogged to the axletrees,
    Or ploughing the sodden loam.

And then when the roads are at their worst,
    The bushman's children hear
The cruel blows of the whips reversed
While bullocks pull as their hearts would burst,
    And bellow with pain and fear.

And thus—with glimpses of home and rest—
    Are the long, long journeys done;
And thus—'tis a thankless life at the best—
Is distance fought in the mighty West,
    And the lonely battles won.

[*1889*]

Middleton's Rouseabout

T all and freckled and sandy,
    Face of a country lout;
This was the picture of Andy,
    Middleton's Rouseabout.

Type of a coming nation,
  In the land of cattle and sheep,
Worked on Middleton's station,
  "Pound a week and his keep".

On Middleton's wide dominions
  Plied the stockwhip and shears;
Hadn't any opinions,
  Hadn't any "idears".

Swiftly the years went over,
  Liquor and drought prevailed;
Middleton went as a drover
  After his station had failed.

Type of a careless nation,
  Men who are soon played out,
Middleton was:—and his station
  Was bought by the Rouseabout.

Flourishing beard and sandy,
  Tall and solid and stout:
This is the picture of Andy,
  Middleton's Rouseabout.

Now on his own dominions
  Works with his overseers;
Hasn't any opinions,
  Hasn't any idears.

[March 1890]

25

The Glass on the Bar

T hree bushmen one morning rode up to an inn,
  And one of them called for the drinks with a grin;
They'd only returned from a trip to the North,
And, eager to greet them, the landlord came forth.
He absently poured out a glass of Three Star,
And set down that drink with the rest on the bar.

"There, that is for Harry," he said, "and it's queer,
'Tis the very same glass that he drank from last year;
His name's on the glass, you can read it like print,
He scratched it himself with an old piece of flint;
I remember his drink—it was always Three Star"—
And the landlord looked out through the door of the bar.

He looked at the horses, and counted but three:
"You were always together—where's Harry?" cried he.
O sadly they looked at the glass as they said,
"You may put it away, for our old mate is dead;"
But one, gazing out o'er the ridges afar,
Said, "We owe him a shout—leave the glass on the bar."

They thought of the far-away grave on the plain,
They thought of the comrade who came not again,
They lifted their glasses, and sadly they said:
"We drink to the name of the mate who is dead."
And the sunlight streamed in, and a light like a star
Seemed to glow in the depth of the glass on the bar.

And still in that shanty a tumbler is seen,
It stands by the clock, ever polished and clean;

And often the strangers will read as they pass
The name of a bushman engraved on the glass;
And though on the shelf but a dozen there are,
That glass never stands with the rest on the bar.

[*Sydney, April 1890*]

The Pavement Stones

A SONG OF THE UNEMPLOYED

When first I came to town, resolved
   To fight my way alone,
No prouder foot than mine e'er trod
   Upon the pavement stone;
But I am one in thousands,
   And why should I repine?
The pavement stones have broken springs
   In stronger feet than mine.

I brought to aid me all the hope
   And energy of youth;
And in my heart I felt the strength
   Of plain bucolic truth:
The independence nourished
   Amid the hills and trees—
But, ah! the city hath a cure
   For qualities like these.

I wonder oft how e'er I made
　　The efforts that I made,
For after three long weary years
　　I taught myself a trade.
And two more years and I was free
　　With strength and hope elate,
For "he that hath a trade," they say,
　　"Hath also an estate."

I tramped the streets and looked for work
　　And begged for work in vain,
Until I recked not, though I ne'er
　　Might touch my tools again.
I tramped the streets despairing;
　　My cheeks grew white and thin;
I felt the pavement wearing through
　　The leather, sock, and skin.

The bitter war goes on between
　　The idlers and the drones,
Until the hearts of men grow cold
　　And hard as pavement stones;
But I am one amid the crowd,
　　Then why should I repine?
The pavement stones have broken springs
　　In stronger feet than mine.

[1890—November?]

28

The Statue of our Queen

Pride, selfishness in every line,
  And on its face a frown,
It stands, a sceptre in its hand,
  And points forever down.
And who will kneel? The unemployed!
  Small homage pay, I ween,
The only men who gather 'neath
  The Statue of our Queen.

I'd scarcely wonder if the sun,
  That rises with good grace,
Should sink and leave the day undone
  At sight of such a face.
But no! The day will still have birth
  In all its golden sheen,
When antiquarians unearth
  The Statue of our Queen.

Then if you'd have us loyal bide
  As we have loyal been,
Great Parkes! for love of England, hide
  The Statue of our Queen.

[1890?]

29

Dan Wasn't Thrown From His Horse

T hey say he was thrown and run over,
  But that is sheer nonsense, of course:
I taught him to ride when a kiddy,
  And Dan wasn't thrown from his horse.

The horse that Dan rode was a devil—
  The kind of a brute I despise,
With nasty white eyelashes fringing
  A pair of red, sinister eyes.

And a queerly-shaped spot on his forehead,
  Where I put a conical ball
The day that he murdered Dan Denver,
  The pluckiest rider of all.

'Twas after the races were over
  And Duggan (a Talbragar man)
And two of the Denvers, and Barney
  Were trying a gallop with Dan.

Dan's horse on a sudden got vicious,
  And reared up an' plunged in the race,
Then threw back his head, hitting Dan like
  A sledge-hammer, full in the face.

Dan stopped and got down, stood a moment,
  Then fell to the ground like a stone,
And died about ten minutes after;
  But they're liars who say he was thrown.

[May? 1891]

30

Freedom on the Wallaby

Our fathers toiled for bitter bread
    While idlers thrived beside them;
But food to eat and clothes to wear
    Their native land denied them.
They left their native land in spite
    Of royalties' regalia,
And so they came, or if they stole
    Were sent out to Australia.

They struggled hard to make a home,
    Hard grubbing 'twas and clearing.
They weren't troubled much with toffs
    When they were pioneering;
And now that we have made the land
    A garden full of promise,
Old greed must crook his dirty hand
    And come to take it from us.

But Freedom's on the Wallaby,
    She'll knock the tyrants silly,
She's going to light another fire
    And boil another billy.
We'll make the tyrants feel the sting
    Of those that they would throttle;
They needn't say the fault is ours
    If blood should stain the wattle.

[Brisbane, May 1891]

31

When the Irish Flag Went By

'Twas eight-hour day, and proudly
   Old Labour led the way;
The drums were beating loudly,
   The crowded streets were gay;
But something touched my heart like pain,
   I could not check the sigh
That rose within my bosom when
   The Irish flag went by.

Bright flags were raised about it
   And one of them my own;
And patriots trod beneath it—
   But it seemed all alone.
I thought of ruined Ireland
   While crystals from the sky
Fell soft like tears by angels shed,
   As the Irish flag went by.

I love the dark green standard
   As Irish patriots do;
It waves above the rebels,
   And I'm a rebel too.
I thought of Ireland's darkest years,
   Her griefs that follow fast;
For drooping as 'twere drenched with tears
   The Irish flag went past.

And though 'twas not in Erin
  That my forefathers trod;
And though my wandering footsteps
  Ne'er pressed the "dear old sod",
I felt the wrongs the Irish feel
  Beneath the northern sky,
And felt the rebel in my heart
  When the Irish flag went by.

I tell you, men of England,
  Who rule the land by might;
I tell you, Irish traitors
  Who sell the sons of light,
That tyranny shall fail at last,
  That changeful days are nigh;
And you shall dip your red flag yet,
  When the Irish flag goes by.

[*Sydney, October 1891*]

The English Queen

I am back from up the country—very sorry that I went—
Seeking for the Southern poets' land whereon to pitch my tent;
I have lost a lot of idols, which were broken on the track,
Burnt a lot of fancy verses, and I'm glad that I am back.
Further out may be the pleasant scenes of which our poets boast,
But I think the country's rather more inviting round the coast.

33

Anyway, I'll stay at present at a boarding-house in town,
Drinking beer and lemon-squashes, taking baths and
    cooling down.

"Sunny plains!" Great Scott!—those burning wastes of barren soil
    and sand
With their everlasting fences stretching out across the land!
Desolation where the crow is! Desert where the eagle flies,
Paddocks where the luny bullock starts and stares with
    reddened eyes;
Where, in clouds of dust enveloped, roasted bullock-drivers creep
Slowly past the sun-dried shepherd dragged behind his
    crawling sheep.
Stunted peak of granite gleaming, glaring like a molten mass
Turned from some infernal furnace on a plain devoid of grass.

Miles and miles of thirsty gutters—strings of muddy water-holes
In the place of "shining rivers"—"walled by cliffs and
    forest boles".
Barren ridges, gullies, ridges! where the everlasting flies—
Fiercer than the plagues of Egypt—swarm about your
    blighted eyes!
Bush! where there is no horizon! where the buried bushman sees
Nothing—Nothing! but the sameness of the ragged, stunted trees!
Lonely hut where drought's eternal—suffocating atmosphere—
Where the God-forgotten hatter dreams of city life and beer.

Treacherous tracks that trap the stranger, endless roads that
    gleam and glare,
Dark and evil-looking gullies, hiding secrets here and there!
Dull dumb flats and stony rises, where the toiling bullocks bake,
And the sinister "gohanna", and the lizard, and the snake.
Land of day and night—no morning freshness, and no afternoon,

When the great white sun in rising brings the summer heat
    in June.
Dismal country for the exile, when the shades begin to fall
From the sad heart-breaking sunset, to the newchum worst of all.

Dreary land in rainy weather, with the endless clouds that drift
O'er the bushman like a blanket that the Lord will never lift—
Dismal land when it is raining—growl of floods, and, O the woosh
Of the rain and wind together on the dark bed of the bush—
Ghastly fires in lonely humpies where the granite rocks are piled
In the rain-swept wildernesses that are wildest of the wild.

Land where gaunt and haggard women live alone and work
    like men,
Till their husbands, gone a-droving, will return to them again:
Homes of men! if homes had ever such a God-forgotten place,
Where the wild selector's children fly before a stranger's face.
Home of tragedy applauded by the dingoes' dismal yell,
Heaven of the shanty-keeper—fitting fiend for such a hell—
And the wallaroos and wombats, and, of course, the
    curlew's call—
And the lone sundowner tramping ever onward through it all!

I am back from up the country, up the country where I went
Seeking for the Southern poets' land whereon to pitch my tent;
I have shattered many idols out along the dusty track,
Burnt a lot of fancy verses—and I'm glad that I am back.
I believe the Southern poets' dream will not be realized
Till the plains are irrigated and the land is humanized.
I intend to stay at present, as I said before, in town
Drinking beer and lemon-squashes, taking baths and
    cooling down.

[*Sydney, June-July 1892*]

The City Bushman

It was pleasant up the country, City Bushman, where you went,
For you sought the greener patches and you travelled
   like a gent;
And you curse the trams and buses and the turmoil and the push,
Though you know the squalid city needn't keep you from
   the bush;
But we lately heard you singing of the "plains where
   shade is not",
And you mentioned it was dusty—"all was dry and all was hot."

True, the bush "hath moods and changes"—and the bushman
   hath 'em, too,
For he's not a poet's dummy—he's a man, the same as you;
But his back is growing rounder—slaving for the absentee—
And his toiling wife is thinner than a country wife should be.
For we noticed that the faces of the folks we chanced to meet
Should have made a greater contrast to the faces in the street;
And, in short, we think the bushman's being driven to the wall,
And it's doubtful if his spirit will be "loyal thro' it all".

Though the bush has been romantic and it's nice to sing about,
There's a lot of patriotism that the land could do without—
Sort of BRITISH WORKMAN nonsense that shall perish in the scorn
Of the drover who is driven and the shearer who is shorn—
Of the struggling western farmers who have little time for rest,
And are ruined on selections in the sheep-infested West;
Droving songs are very pretty, but they merit little thanks
From the people of a country in possession of the Banks.

And the "rise and fall of seasons" suits the rise and fall of rhyme,

36

But we know that western seasons do not run on schedule time;
For the drought will go on drying while there's anything to dry,
Then it rains until you'd fancy it would bleach the sunny sky—
Then it pelters out of reason, for the downpour day and night
Nearly sweeps the population to the Great Australian Bight.
It is up in Northern Queensland that the seasons do their best,
But it's doubtful if you ever saw a season in the West;
There are years without an autumn or a winter or a spring,
There are broiling Junes, and summers when it rains
    like anything.

In the bush my ears were opened to the singing of the bird,
But the "carol of the magpie" was a thing I never heard.
Once the beggar roused my slumbers in a shanty, it is true,
But I only heard him asking, "Who the blanky blank are you?"
And the bell-bird in the ranges—but his "silver chime" is harsh
When it's heard beside the solo of the curlew in the marsh.

Yes, I heard the shearers singing "William Riley", out of tune;
Saw 'em fighting round a shanty on a Sunday afternoon;
But the bushman isn't always "trapping brumbies in the night",
Nor is he for ever riding when "the morn is fresh and bright",
And he isn't always singing in the humpies on the run—
And the camp-fire's "cheery blazes" are a trifle overdone;
We have grumbled with the bushmen round the fire on rainy days,
When the smoke would blind a bullock and there wasn't any blaze,
Save the blazes of our language, for we cursed the fire in turn
Till the atmosphere was heated and the wood began to burn.
Then we had to wring our blueys which were rotting in the swags,
And we saw the sugar leaking through the bottoms of the bags,
And we couldn't raise a chorus, for the toothache and the cramp,
While we spent the hours of darkness draining puddles
    round the camp.

Would you like to change with Clancy—go a-droving? tell us true,
For we rather think that Clancy would be glad to change with you,
And be something in the city; but 'twould give your muse a shock
To be losing time and money through the foot-rot in the flock,
And you wouldn't mind the beauties underneath the starry dome
If you had a wife and children and a lot of bills at home.

Did you ever guard the cattle when the night was inky-black,
And it rained, and icy water trickled gently down your back
Till your saddle-weary backbone fell a-aching to the roots
And you almost felt the croaking of the bull-frog in your boots—
Sit and shiver in the saddle, curse the restless stock and cough
Till a squatter's nameless dummy cantered up to warn you off?
Did you fight the drought and pleuro when the "seasons"
     were asleep,
Felling sheoaks all the morning for a flock of starving sheep,
Drinking mud instead of water—climbing trees and
     lopping boughs
For the broken-hearted bullocks and the dry and dusty cows?

Do you think the bush was better in the "good old droving days",
When the squatter ruled supremely as the king of western ways,
When you got a slip of paper for the little you could earn,
But were forced to take provisions from the station in return—
When you couldn't keep a chicken at your humpy on the run,
For the squatter wouldn't let you—and your work was never done;
When you had to leave the missus in a lonely hut forlorn
While you "rose up Willy Riley"—in the days ere you were born?

Ah! we read about the drovers and the shearers and the like
Till we wonder why such happy and romantic fellows strike.
Don't you fancy that the poets ought to give the bush a rest
Ere they raise a just rebellion in the over-written West?

Where the simple-minded bushman gets a meal and bed and rum
Just by riding round reporting phantom flocks that never come;
Where the scalper—never troubled by the "war-whoop
     of the push"—
Has a quiet little billet—breeding rabbits in the bush;
Where the idle shanty-keeper never fails to make a "draw",
And the dummy gets his tucker through provisions in the law;
Where the labour-agitator—when the shearers rise in might—
Makes his money sacrificing all his substance for The Right;
Where the squatter makes his fortune, and "the seasons
     rise and fall",
And the poor and honest bushman has to suffer for it all;
Where the drovers and the shearers and the bushmen and the rest
Never reach the Eldorado of the poets of the West.

And you think the bush is purer and that life is better there,
But it doesn't seem to pay you like the "squalid street
     and square".
Pray inform us, City Bushman, where you read, in prose or verse,
Of the awful "city urchin who would greet you with a curse".
There are golden hearts in gutters, though their owners
     lack the fat,
And we'll back a teamster's offspring to outswear a city brat.

Do you think we're never jolly where the trams and buses rage?
Did you head the gods in chorus when "Ri-tooral" held the stage?
Did you catch a ring of sorrow in the city urchin's voice
When he yelled for Billy Elton, when he thumped the floor
     for Royce?
Do the bushmen, down on pleasure, miss the everlasting stars
When they drink and flirt and so on in the glow of private bars?
You've a down on "trams and buses", or the "roar" of 'em,
     you said,

And the "filthy, dirty attic", where you never toiled for bread.
(And about that self-same attic—Lord! wherever have you been?
For the struggling needlewoman mostly keeps her attic clean.)
But you'll find it very jolly with the cuff-and-collar push,
And the city seems to suit you, while you rave about the bush.

You'll admit that Up-the-Country, more especially in drought,
Isn't quite the Eldorado that the poets rave about,
Yet at times we long to gallop where the reckless bushman rides
In the wake of startled brumbies that are flying for their hides;
Long to feel the saddle tremble once again between our knees
And to hear the stockwhips rattle just like rifles in the trees!
Long to feel the bridle-leather tugging strongly in the hand
And to feel once more a little like a "native of the land".
And the ring of bitter feeling in the jingling of our rhymes
Isn't suited to the country nor the spirit of the times.
Let us go together droving, and returning, if we live,
Try to understand each other while we reckon up the "div".

[*July 1892*]

The Grog-an'-Grumble Steeplechase

'Twixt the coastline and the border lay the town of Grog-an'-Grumble
In the days before the bushman was a dull 'n' heartless drudge,

40

An' they say the local meeting was a drunken rough-and-tumble,
    Which was ended pretty often by an inquest on the judge.
An' 'tis said the city talent very often caught a tartar
    In the Grog-an'-Grumble sportsman, 'n' retired with
        broken heads,
For the fortune, life, and safety of the Grog-an'-Grumble starter
    Mostly hung upon the finish of the local thoroughbreds.

Pat M'Durmer was the owner of a horse they called the Screamer,
    Which he called the "quickest shtepper 'twixt the Darling
        and the sea";
And I think it's very doubtful if the stomach-troubled dreamer
    Ever saw a more outrageous piece of equine scenery;
For his points were most decided, from his end to his beginning,
    He had eyes of different colour, and his legs they wasn't mates.
Pat M'Durmer said he always came "widin a flip av winnin' ",
    An' his sire had come from England, 'n' his dam was from
        the States.

Friends would argue with M'Durmer, and they said he was
        in error
    To put up his horse the Screamer, for he'd lose in any case,
And they said a city racer by the name of Holy Terror
    Was regarded as the winner of the coming steeplechase;
But he said he had the knowledge to come in when it was raining,
    And irrelevantly mentioned that he knew the time of day,
So he rose in their opinion. It was noticed that the training
    Of the Screamer was conducted in a dark mysterious way.

Well, the day arrived in glory; 'twas a day of jubilation
    With careless-hearted bushmen for a hundred miles around,
An' the rum 'n' beer 'n' whisky came in waggons from the station,
    An' the Holy Terror talent were the first upon the ground.

41

Judge M'Ard—with whose opinion it was scarcely safe
    to wrestle—
  Took his dangerous position on the bark-and-sapling stand:
He was what the local Stiggins used to speak of as a "wessel
    Of wrath", and he'd a bludgeon that he carried in his hand.

"Off ye go!" the starter shouted, as down fell a stupid jockey—
  Off they started in disorder—left the jockey where he lay—
And they fell and rolled and galloped down the crooked course
    and rocky,
  Till the pumping of the Screamer could be heard a mile away.
But he kept his legs and galloped; he was used to rugged courses,
  And he lumbered down the gully till the ridge began to quake:
And he ploughed along the siding, raising earth till other horses
  An' their riders, too, were blinded by the dust-cloud in his wake.

From the ruck he'd struggled slowly—they were much surprised
    to find him
  Close abeam of Holy Terror as along the flat they tore—
Even higher still and denser rose the cloud of dust behind him,
  While in more divided splinters flew the shattered rails before.
"Terror!" "Dead heat!" they were shouting—"Terror!" but the
    Screamer hung out
  Nose to nose with Holy Terror as across the creek they swung,
An' M'Durmer shouted loudly, "Put yer tongue out! put yer
    tongue out!"
  An' the Screamer put his tongue out, and he won by
    half-a-tongue.

[*1892*]

42

When Your Pants Begin to Go

W hen you wear a cloudy collar and a shirt that isn't white,
  And you cannot sleep for thinking how you'll reach
   tomorrow night,
You may be a man of sorrows, and on speaking terms with Care,
But as yet you're unacquainted with the Demon of Despair;
For I rather think that nothing heaps the trouble on your mind
Like the knowledge that your trousers badly need a patch behind.

I have noticed when misfortune strikes the hero of the play
That his clothes are worn and tattered in a most unlikely way;
And the gods applaud and cheer him while he whines and
     loafs around,
And they never seem to notice that his pants are mostly sound;
But, of course, he cannot help it, for our mirth would mock
     his care,
If the ceiling of his trousers showed the patches of repair.

You are none the less a hero if you elevate your chin
When you feel the pavement wearing through the leather, sock,
     and skin;
You are rather more heroic than are ordinary folk
If you scorn to fish for pity under cover of a joke;
You will face the doubtful glances of the people that you know;
But—of course, you're bound to face them when your pants
     begin to go.

If, when flush, you took your pleasures—failed to make a god
     of Pelf,

43

Some will say that for your troubles you can only thank yourself;
Some will swear you'll die a beggar, but you only laugh at that
While your garments hang together and you wear a decent hat;
You may laugh at their predictions while your soles are wearing
    through,
But—a man's an awful coward when his pants are going too.

Though the present and the future may be anything but bright,
It is best to tell the fellows that you're getting on all right.
And a man prefers to say it—'tis a manly lie to tell,
For the folks may be persuaded that you're doing very well;
But it's hard to be a hero, and it's hard to wear a grin,
When your most important garment is in places very thin.

Get some sympathy and comfort from the chum who knows
    you best,
That your sorrows won't run over in the presence of the rest;
There's a chum that you can go to when you feel inclined
    to whine;
He'll declare your coat is tidy, and he'll say: "Just look at mine!"
Though you may be patched all over he will say it doesn't show,
And he'll swear it can't be noticed when your pants begin to go.

Brother mine, and of misfortune! times are hard, but do not fret,
Keep your courage up and struggle, and we'll laugh at these
    things yet.
Though there is no corn in Egypt, surely Africa has some—
Keep your smile in working order for the better days to come!
We shall often laugh together at the hard times that we know,
And get measured by the tailor when our pants begin to go.

Now the lady of refinement, in the lap of comfort rocked,
Chancing on these rugged verses, will pretend that she is shocked.

Leave her to her smelling-bottle; 'tis the wealthy who decide
That the world should hide its patches 'neath the cruel cloak
  of pride;
And I think there's something noble, and I'll swear there's
  nothing low,
In the pride of Human Nature when its pants begin to go.

[*1892*]

The Morning of
New Zealand

I n the morning of New Zealand we should sing a Marseillaise!
   We should sing a hymn of triumph, we should sing a song
  of praise!
For our women are ennobled! The narrow days are o'er,
And the Fathers of New Zealand shall be famous evermore.

Men, you cannot comprehend it! Men, you do not understand
That the actions of your leaders have immortalized the land!
For the filthy gods of ages from our shoulders shall be hurled,
And the influence of women revolutionize the world!

Many years may pass in error ere the nations realize;
And the South awhile is silent with the silence of surprise;
But the victories are coming, and the tribute is to come
In a roar of exultation from the hearts of Christendom.

'Tis the glory of New Zealand that her sons were first to see
That there never was a free land where the women were not free!
Time shall hear the nations asking why it was not ever thus,
For the freedom of our women comes with liberty to us.

[Wellington, N.Z., December 1893]

Lake Eliza

T he sand was heavy on our feet,
　A Christmas sky was o'er us,
And half a mile through dust and heat
　Lake 'Liza lay before us.
"You'll have a long and heavy tramp"—
　So said the last adviser—
"You can't do better than to camp
　To-night at Lake Eliza."

We quite forgot our aching shanks,
　A cheerful spirit caught us;
We thought of green and shady banks,
　We thought of pleasant waters.
'Neath sky as niggard of its rain
　As of his gold the miser,
By mulga scrub and lignum plain
　We'd tramped to Lake Eliza.

A patch of grey discoloured sand,
    A fringe of tufty grasses,
A lonely pub in mulga scrub
    Is all the stranger passes.
He'd pass the Lake a dozen times
    And yet be none the wiser;
I hope that I shall never be
    As dry as Lake Eliza.

No patch of green or water seen
    To cheer the weary plodder;
The grass is tough as fencing-wire,
    And just as good for fodder.
And when I see it mentioned in
    Some local ADVERTISER,
'Twill make me laugh, or make me grin—
    The name of "Lake Eliza".

[1893]

Out Back

The old year went, and the new returned, in the withering
    weeks of drought,
The cheque was spent that the shearer earned, and the sheds were
    all cut out;
The publican's words were short and few, and the publican's looks
    were black—

And the time had come, as the shearer knew, to carry his swag
Out Back.

*For time means tucker, and tramp you must, where the scrubs and
plains are wide,*
*With seldom a track that a man can trust, or a mountain peak
to guide;*
All day long in the dust and heat—when summer is on the track—
*With stinted stomachs and blistered feet, they carry their swags
Out Back.*

He tramped away from the shanty there, when the days were
long and hot,
With never a soul to know or care if he died on the track or not.
The poor of the city have friends in woe, no matter how much
they lack,
But only God and the swagmen know how a poor man fares
Out Back.

He begged his way on the parched Paroo and the Warrego tracks
once more,
And lived like a dog, as the swagmen do, till the Western
stations shore;
But men were many, and sheds were full, for work in the town
was slack—
The traveller never got hands in wool, though he tramped for a
year Out Back.

In stifling noons when his back was wrung by its load, and the air
seemed dead,
And the water warmed in the bag that hung to his aching arm
like lead,
Or in times of flood, when plains were seas, and the scrubs were
cold and black,

He ploughed in mud to his trembling knees, and paid for his sins
　　Out Back.

He blamed himself in the year "Too Late" for the wreck of his
　　strong young life,
And no one dreamed but a shearing-mate 'twas the fault of his
　　faithless wife;
There are times when wrongs from your kindred come, and
　　treacherous tongues attack—
When a man is better away from home, and dead to the world,
　　Out Back.

And dirty and careless and old he wore, as his lamp of hope
　　grew dim;
He tramped for years till the swag he bore seemed part of himself
　　to him.
As a bullock drags in the sandy ruts, he followed the dreary track,
With never a thought but to reach the huts when the sun went
　　down Out Back.

It chanced one day, when the north wind blew in his face like a
　　furnace-breath,
He left the track for a tank he knew—'twas a shorter cut to death;
For the bed of the tank was hard and dry, and crossed with many
　　a crack,
And O it's a terrible thing to die of thirst in the scrub Out Back.

A drover came, but the fringe of law was eastward many a mile;
He never reported the thing he saw, for it was not worth his while.
The tanks are full and the grass is high in the mulga off the track,
Where the bleaching bones of a white man lie by his mouldering
　　swag Out Back.

For times means tucker, and tramp they must, where the plains and
    scrubs are wide,
With seldom a track that a man can trust, or a mountain peak
    to guide;
All day long in the flies and heat the men of the outside track
With stinted stomachs and blistered feet must carry their swags
    Out Back.

I'll Tell You What, You Wanderers

I 'll tell you what, you wanderers, who drift from town to town;
Don't look into a good girl's eyes, until you've settled down.
It's hard to go away alone and leave old chums behind—
It's hard to travel steerage when your tastes are more refined—
To reach a place when times are bad, and to be stranded there,
No money in your pocket nor a decent rag to wear.
But to be forced from that fond clasp, from that last
    clinging kiss—
By poverty! There is on earth no harder thing than this.

[*December 1894*]

Reedy River

T en miles down Reedy River
A pool of water lies,
And all the year it mirrors
The changes in the skies,
And in that pool's broad bosom
Is room for all the stars;
Its bed of sand has drifted
O'er countless rocky bars.

Around the lower edges
There waves a bed of reeds,
Where water rats are hidden
And where the wild duck breeds;
And grassy slopes rise gently
To ridges long and low,
Where groves of wattle flourish
And native bluebells grow.

Beneath the granite ridges
The eye may just discern
Where Rocky Creek emerges
From deep green banks of fern;
And standing tall between them,
The grassy sheoaks cool
The hard, blue-tinted waters
Before they reach the pool.

Ten miles down Reedy River
One Sunday afternoon,
I rode with Mary Campbell

To that broad bright lagoon;
We left our horses grazing
    Till shadows climbed the peak,
And strolled beneath the sheoaks
    On the banks of Rocky Creek.

Then home along the river
    That night we rode a race,
And the moonlight lent a glory
    To Mary Campbell's face;
And I pleaded for my future
    All thro' that moonlight ride,
Until our weary horses
    Drew closer side by side.

Ten miles from Ryan's crossing
    And five below the peak,
I built a little homestead
    On the banks of Rocky Creek;
I cleared the land and fenced it
    And ploughed the rich red loam,
And my first crop was golden
    When I brought Mary home.

Now still down Reedy River
    The grassy sheoaks sigh,
And the waterholes still mirror
    The pictures in the sky;
And over all for ever
    Go sun and moon and stars,
While the golden sand is drifting
    Across the rocky bars;

But of the hut I builded
　　There are no traces now,
And many rains have levelled
　　The furrows of the plough;
And my bright days are olden,
　　For the twisted branches wave
And the wattle blossoms golden
　　On the hill by Mary's grave.

[*1896—May?*]

The Men Who Come Behind

There's a class of men (and women) who are always on their
　　guard—
Cunning, treacherous, suspicious—feeling softly—grasping hard—
Brainy, yet without the courage to forsake the beaten track—
Cautiously they feel their way behind a bolder spirit's back.

If you save a bit of money, and you start a little store—
Say, an oyster-shop, for instance, where there wasn't one before—
When the shop begins to pay you, and the rent is off your mind,
You will see another started by a chap that comes behind.

So it is, and so it might have been, my friend, with me and you—
When a friend of both and neither interferes between the two;

They will fight like fiends, forgetting in their passion mad
    and blind,
That the row is mostly started by the folk who come behind.

They will stick to you like sin will, while your money comes
    and goes,
But they'll leave you when you haven't got a shilling in your
    clothes.
You may get some help above you, but you'll nearly always find
That you cannot get assistance from the men who come behind.

There are many, far too many, in the world of prose and rhyme,
Always looking for another's "footsteps on the sands of time".
Journalistic imitators are the meanest of mankind;
And the grandest themes are hackneyed by the pens that
    come behind.

If you strike a novel subject, write it up, and do not fail,
They will rhyme and prose about it till your very own is stale,
As they raved about the region that the wattle-boughs perfume
Till the reader cursed the bushman and the stink of wattle-bloom.

They will follow in your footsteps while you're groping for
    the light;
But they'll run to get before you when they see you're going right;
And they'll trip you up and baulk you in their blind and
    greedy heat,
Like a stupid pup that hasn't learned to trail behind your feet.

Take your loads of sin and sorrow on more energetic backs!
Go and strike across the country where there are not any tracks!
And—we fancy that the subject could be further treated here,
But we'll leave it to be hackneyed by the fellows in the rear.

[*1896*]

The Uncultured Rhymer to his Cultured Critics

F ight through ignorance, want, and care—
  Through the griefs that crush the spirit;
Push your way to a fortune fair,
  And the smiles of the world you'll merit.
Long, as a boy, for the chance to learn—
  For the chance that Fate denies you;
Win degrees where the Life-lights burn,
  And scores will teach and advise you.

My cultured friends! you have come too late
  With your bypath nicely graded;
I've fought thus far on my track of Fate,
  And I'll follow the rest unaided.
Must I be stopped by a college gate
  On the track of Life encroaching?
Be dumb to Love, and be dumb to Hate,
  For the lack of a college coaching?

You grope for Truth in a language dead—
  In the dust 'neath tower and steeple!
What know you of the tracks we tread?
  And what know you of our people?
"I must read this, and that, and the rest,"
  And write as the cult expects me?—
I'll read the book that may please me best,
  And write as my heart directs me!

You were quick to pick on a faulty line
  That I strove to put my soul in:
Your eyes were keen for a "dash" of mine
  In the place of a semi-colon—
And blind to the rest. And is it for such
  As you I must brook restriction?
"I was taught too little?" I learnt too much
  To care for a pedant's diction!

Must I turn aside from my destined way
  For a task your Joss would find me?
I come with strength of the living day,
  And with half the world behind me;
I leave you alone in your cultured halls
  To drivel and croak and cavil:
Till your voice goes further than college walls,
  Keep out of the tracks we travel!

[*February 1897*]

The Old Bark School

I t was built of bark and poles, and the floor was full of holes
  Where each leak in rainy weather made a pool;
And the walls were mostly cracks lined with calico and sacks—
  There was little need for windows in the school.

Then we rode to school and back by the rugged gully track
  On the old grey horse that carried three or four;

56

And he looked so very wise that he lit the master's eyes
   Every time he put his head in at the door.

He had run with Cobb and Co.—"that grey leader, let him go!"
   There were men "as knowed the brand upon his hide,"
And "as knowed it on the course" . . . . Funeral service:
    "Good old horse!"
   When we burnt him in the gully where he died.

And the master thought the same. 'Twas from Ireland that
    he came,
   Where the tanks are full all summer, and the feed is
    simply grand;
And the joker then in vogue said his lessons wid a brogue—
   'Twas unconscious imitation, let the reader understand.

And we learnt the world in scraps from some ancient dingy maps
   Long discarded by the public-schools in town;
And as nearly every book dated back to Captain Cook
   Our geography was somewhat upside-down.

It was "in the book" and so—well, at that we'd let it go,
   For we never would believe that print could lie;
And we all learnt pretty soon that when we came out at noon
   "The sun is in the south part of the sky."

And Ireland! *that* was known from the coast-line to Athlone:
   We got little information *re* the land that gave us birth;
Save that Captain Cook was killed (and was very likely grilled)
   And "the natives of New Holland are the lowest race on earth."

And a woodcut, in its place, of the same degraded race
   Seemed a lot more like a camel than the blackfellows we knew;

Jimmy Bullock, with the rest, scratched his head and gave it best;
　　But his faith was sadly shaken by a bobtailed kangaroo.

But the old bark-school is gone, and the spot it stood upon
　　Is a cattle-camp in winter where the curlew's cry is heard;
There's a brick-school on the flat, but a schoolmate teaches that,
　　For, about the time they built it, our old master was
　　　"transferred".

But the bark-school comes again with exchanges 'cross the plain—
　　With the OUT-BACK ADVERTISER; and my fancy roams at large
When I read of passing stock, of a western mob or flock,
　　With "James Bullock", "Grey", or "Henry Dale" in charge.

And I think how Jimmy went from the old bark school content,
　　With his "eddication" finished, with his pack-horse after him;
And perhaps if I were back I would take the self-same track,
　　For I wish my learning ended when the Master "finished" Jim.

[1897?]

The Old Jimmy Woodser

The old Jimmy Woodser comes into the bar,
　　Unwelcomed, unnoticed, unknown,
Too old and too odd to be drunk with, by far;
And he glides to the end where the lunch baskets are
　　And they say that he tipples alone.

His frock-coat is green and the nap is no more,
    And the style of his hat is at rest.
He wears the peaked collar our grandfathers wore,
The black-ribboned tie that was legal of yore,
    And the coat buttoned over his breast.

When first he came in, for a moment I thought
    That my vision or wits were astray;
For a picture and page out of Dickens he brought,
'Twas an old file dropped in from the Chancery Court
    To a wine-vault just over the way.

But I dreamed as he tasted his bitters to-night,
    And the lights in the bar-room grew dim,
That the shades of the friends of that other day's light,
And of girls that were bright in our grandfathers' sight,
    Lifted shadowy glasses to him.

And I opened the door as the old man passed out,
    With his short, shuffling step and bowed head;
And I sighed, for I felt as I turned me about,
An odd sense of respect—born of whisky no doubt—
    For the life that was fifty years dead.

And I thought—there are times when our memory trends
    Through the future, as 'twere, on its own—
That I, out of date ere my pilgrimage ends,
In a new fashioned bar to dead loves and dead friends
    Might drink like the old man alone:
    While they whisper, "He boozes alone."

[*1899?*]

59

Second Class Wait Here

O n suburban railway stations—you may see them as you
pass—
There are signboards on the platforms saying, "Wait here
second class";
And to me the whirr and thunder and the cluck of running gear
Seem to be for ever saying, saying "Second class wait here"—
    "Wait here second class,
    Second class wait here."
Seem to be for ever saying, saying "Second class wait here".

And the second class were waiting in the days of serf and prince,
And the second class are waiting—they've been waiting ever since.
There are gardens in the background, and the line is bare
    and drear,
Yet they wait beneath a signboard, sneering "Second class
    wait here".

I have waited oft in winter, in the mornings dark and damp,
When the asphalt platform glistened underneath the lonely lamp.
Ghastly on the brick-faced cutting "Sellum's Soap" and
    "Blower's Beer";
Ghastly on enamelled signboards with their "Second class
    wait here".

And the others seemed like burglars, slouched and muffled
    to the throats,
Standing round apart and silent in their shoddy overcoats,
And the wind among the wires, and the poplars bleak and bare,
Seemed to be for ever snarling, snarling "Second class wait there".

Out beyond the further suburb, 'neath a chimney stack alone,
Lay the works of Grinder Brothers, with a platform of their own;
And I waited there and suffered, waited there for many a year,
Slaved beneath a phantom signboard, telling our class
   to wait here.

Ah! a man must feel revengeful for a boyhood such as mine.
God! I hate the very houses near the workshop by the line;
And the smell of railway stations, and the roar of running gear,
And the scornful-seeming signboards, saying "Second class
   wait here".

There's a train with Death for driver, which is ever going past,
And there are no class compartments, and we all must go at last
To the long white jasper platform with an Eden in the rear;
And there won't be any signboards, saying "Second class
   wait here".

[*1899?*]

The Sliprails and the Spur

T he colours of the setting sun
   Withdrew across the Western land—
He raised the sliprails, one by one,
   And shot them home with trembling hand;
Her brown hands clung—her face grew pale—
   Ah! quivering chin and eyes that brim!—

One quick, fierce kiss across the rail,
    And, "Good-bye, Mary!" "Good-bye, Jim!"

> *O he rides hard to race the pain*
> > *Who rides from love, who rides from home;*
> *But he rides slowly home again,*
> > *Whose heart has learnt to love and roam.*

A hand upon the horse's mane,
    And one foot in the stirrup set,
And, stooping back to kiss again,
    With "Good-bye, Mary! don't you fret!
When I come back"—he laughed for her—
    "We do not know how soon 'twill be;
I'll whistle as I round the spur—
    You let the sliprails down for me."

She gasped for sudden loss of hope,
    As, with a backward wave to her,
He cantered down the grassy slope
    And swiftly round the dark'ning spur.
Black-pencilled panels standing high,
    And darkness fading into stars,
And blurring fast against the sky,
    A faint white form beside the bars.

And often at the set of sun,
    In winter bleak and summer brown,
She'd steal across the little run,
    And shyly let the sliprails down,
And listen there when darkness shut
    The nearer spur in silence deep;
And when they called her from the hut
    Steal home and cry herself to sleep.

A great white gate where sliprails were,
A brick house 'neath the mountain brow,
The "mad girl" buried by the spur
So long ago, forgotten now.

And he rides hard to dull the pain
Who rides from one that loves him best;
And he rides slowly back again
Whose restless heart must rove for rest.

[*1899*]

The Rush to London

You're off away to London now,
Where no one dare ignore you,
With Southern laurels on your brow,
And all the world before you.
But if you should return again,
Forgotten and unknowing,
Then one shall wait in wind and rain,
Where forty cheered you going.

You're off away to London, proved,
Where fair girls shall adore you;
The poor, plain face of one that loved
May never rise before you.
But if you should return again,

When young blood ceases flowing,
Then one shall wait in wind and rain,
Where forty cheered you going.

It may be carelessly you spoke
Of never more returning,
But sometimes in the London smoke,
You'll smell the gum leaves burning;
And think of how the grassy plain
Beyond the fog is flowing,
And one that waits in shine or rain,
Where forty cheered you going.

[*1900?*]

The Shearers

No church-bell rings them from the Track,
No pulpit lights their blindness—
'Tis hardship, drought and homelessness
That teach those Bushmen kindness:
The mateship born of barren lands,
Of toil and thirst and danger—
The camp-fare for the stranger set,
The first place to the stranger.

They do the best they can to-day—
Take no thought of the morrow;
Their way is not the old-world way—

They live to lend and borrow.
When shearing's done and cheques gone wrong,
    They call it "time to slither"—
They saddle up and say "So-long!"
    And ride—the Lord knows whither.

And though he may be brown or black,
    Or wrong man there or right man,
The mate that's honest to his mates
    They call that man a "white man"!
They tramp in mateship side by side—
    The Protestant and "Roman"—
They call no biped lord or "sir",
    And touch their hats to no man!

They carry in their swags, perhaps,
    A portrait and a letter—
And, maybe, deep down in their hearts,
    The hope of "something better".
Where lonely miles are long to ride,
    And all days seem recurrent,
There's lots of time to think of men
    They might have been—but weren't.

They turn their faces to the west
    And leave the world behind them—
(Their drought-dried graves are seldom green
    Where even mates can find them).
They know too little of the world
    To rise to wealth or greatness:
But in this book of mine I pay
    My tribute to their straightness.

[1901]

65

The Separation

W e knew too little of the world,
  And you and I were good—
'Twas paltry things that wrecked our lives
  As well I knew they would.
The people said our love was dead,
  But how were they to know?
Ah! had we loved each other less
  We'd not have quarrelled so.

We knew too little of the world,
  And you and I were kind:
We listened to what others said
  And both of us were blind.
The people said 'twas selfishness,
  But how were they to know?
Ah! had we both more selfish been
  We'd not have parted so.

But still when all seems lost on earth
  Then heaven sets a sign—
Kneel down beside your lonely bed,
  And I will kneel by mine,
And let us pray for happy days—
  Like those of long ago.
Ah! had we knelt together then
  We'd not have parted so.

[*1902*]

66

To Hannah

S pirit girl to whom 'twas given
  To revisit scenes of pain,
From the hell I thought was Heaven
  You have lifted me again;
Through the world that I inherit,
  Where I loved her ere she died,
I am walking with the spirit
  Of a dead girl by my side—

Through my old possessions, only
  For a very little while;
And they say that I am lonely,
  And they pity, but I smile:
For the brighter side has won me
  By the calmness that it brings,
And the peace that is upon me
  Does not come of earthly things.

Spirit girl, the good is in me,
  But the flesh you know is weak,
And with no pure soul to win me
  I might miss the path I seek;
Lead me by the love you bore me
  When you trod the earth with me,
Till the light is clear before me
  And my spirit too is free.

[1904—April-May?]

67

To Jim

I gaze upon my son once more,
 With eyes and heart that tire,
As solemnly he stands before
   The screen drawn round the fire;
With hands behind clasped hand in hand,
   Now loosely and now fast—
Just as his fathers used to stand
   For generations past.

A fair and slight and childish form,
   And big brown dreamy eyes—
God help him! for a life of storm
   And strife before him lies:
A wanderer and a gipsy wild,
   I've learnt the world and know,
For I was such another child—
   Ah, many years ago!

But in those dreamy eyes of him
   There is no hint of doubt—
I wish that you could tell me, Jim,
   The things you dream about.
Dream on, and dream the world is true
   And things not what they seem—
'Twill be a bitter day for you
   When wakened from your dream.

You are a child of field and flood,
   But with the gipsy strains
A strong Norwegian sailor's blood

Is running through your veins.
Be true, and slander never stings;
    Be straight, and all may frown—
You'll have the strength to grapple things
    That dragged your father down.

These lines I write with bitter tears
    And failing heart and hand,
But you will read in after years,
    And you will understand:
You'll hear the slander of the crowd,
    They'll whisper tales of shame;
But days will come when you'll be proud
    To bear your father's name.

But O beware of bitterness
    When you are wronged, my lad—
I wish I had the faith in men
    And women that I had!
'Tis better far (for I have felt
    The sadness in my song)
To trust all men and still be wronged
    Than to trust none, and wrong.

Be generous and still do good
    And banish while you live
The spectre of ingratitude
    That haunts the ones who give.
But if the crisis comes at length
    That your future might be marred,
Strike hard, my son, with all your strength!
    For your own self's sake, strike hard!

[June 1904]

69

The King and Queen and I

O Scotty, have you visited the Picture Gallery,
  And did you see the portraits of the King and Queen and me?
The portraits made by Longstaff, and the pictures done by Jack,
Of the King and Queen and Lawson and the lady all in black?

The King is robed in royal state, with medals on his breast,
And like the mother Queen she is Her Majesty is dressed.
The lady's dressed in simple black and sports no precious stones,
And I a suit of reach-me-downs I bought from Davy Jones.

We're strangers two to two, and each unto the other three—
I do not know the lady and I don't think she knows me.
We're strangers to each other here, and to the other two,
And they themselves are strangers yet, if all we hear is true.

I s'pose we're just as satisfied as folks have ever been:
The lady would much rather be her own self than the Queen;
And though I'm down and precious stiff and I admire King Ned,
I'd sooner just be Harry, with his follies on his head.

We four may meet together—stranger folk have met, I ween,
Than a rhymer and a monarch and a lady and a queen.
Ned and I might talk it over on the terrace, frank and free,
With cigars, while Alexandra and the lady's having tea.

Anyway, we'll never quarrel while we're hanging on the wall—
Friends! we all have had our troubles—we are human, one and all!
If by chance we hang together—hang together on the line,—
And the thing should shock the Godly—then it's Longstaff's fault,
    not mine.

[*1905—March?*]

70

The Horseman on the Skyline

W ho's that mysterious rider,
　　Full-sized, yet far away,
Seen by the Western-sider—
　　A spectre of the day?
On ridge or seeming high line
　　Where East the plain expands,
The horseman on the skyline
　　Is known in many lands.

With summer insects drumming
　　And summer skies aglow,
He's there—none saw him coming—
　　He's gone—none saw him go.
Too plain for superstition,
　　Too blurred for one we sought,
He rides across our vision
　　To vanish like a thought.

He never halts nor hurries,
　　But slowly, in broad day,
Along the skyline eastward
　　He seems to pick his way.
He rides against the sunrise,
　　He rides against the gloom,
Where suddenly, in summer,
　　The lurid storm-clouds loom.

He never rides in starlight,
　　Nor underneath the moon,

But often in the distant
  And dazzling haze of noon.
The sad Australian sunset
  (Too sad for pen or tongue)
Has often seen him riding
  Out where the night was young.

On rolling cattle ranches,
  In "country" far away,
Where cowboys took their chances,
  They saw him every day.
And many try to find him
  Where riders never tire—
He leaves no trail behind him
  And never lights a fire.

On run and ranch and veldtland
  He leaves them all in doubt—
A cowboy, or a stockman,
  A horse thief, or a scout.
The glass brings him no nearer,
  Nor hints the way he came;
His features are no clearer,
  He vanishes the same.

Too blurred and dark his clothing
  To hint of his degree;
Inquiries lead to nothing,
  No hoof-marks do we see.
He leaves the watcher puzzled,
  Or leaves the watcher pained:
The horseman on the skyline
  Has never been explained.

Still, where by foot or saddle,
    Or train or motor car,
The people hurry westward—
    It matters not how far—
And, plainly seen by many,
    The greatest and the least—
The rider on the skyline
    Is scouting to the east.

[*1906*]

My Father-in-law and I

My father-in-law is a careworn man,
    And a silent man is he;
But he summons a smile as well as he can
    Whenever he meets with me.
The sign we make with a silent shake
    That speaks of the days gone by—
Like men who meet at a funeral—
    My father-in-law and I.

My father-in-law is a sober man
    (And a virtuous man, I think);
But we spare a shilling whenever we can,
    And we both drop in for a drink.
Our pints they fill, and we say, "Ah, well!"
    With the sound of the world-old sigh—

73

Like the drink that comes after a funeral—
    My father-in-law and I.

My father-in-law is a kindly man—
    A domestic man is he.
He tries to look cheerful as well as he can
    Whenever he meets with me.
But we stand and think till the second drink
    In a silence that might imply
That we'd both get over a funeral,
    My father-in-law and I.

[1906?]

The Gentlemen of Dickens

T he gentlemen of Dickens
    Were mostly very poor,
And innocent of grammar,
    And of parentage obscure;
But rich or poor or thriving,
    Of high or lowly birth,
The gentlemen of Dickens
    Were the grandest on the earth.

The gentlemen of Dickens,
    They wore no fancy names—
Like Reginald or Percy

Fitzgerald or FitzJames;
But names for fools to laugh at,
    That sound like hob-nailed boots,
Like Newman Noggs and Knubbles,
    Toodles and Mr Toots.

They'd little save their kindness,
    Their honesty and truth;
They mostly came embarrassed,
    And stammering and uncouth;
But the gentlemen of Dickens,
    Their women and their girls,
Could speak their minds if need be
    To ladies and to earls.

But one who wore a title
    A lesson, too, could teach:
Lord Feenix—Cousin Feenix
    Of wandering legs and speech.
O he might teach a lesson
    A gentleman could give,
Where he stands by his "lovely
    And accomplished relative".

The gentlemen of Dickens
    Were gamblers now and then
(And looked upon the ladies,
    No doubt, like other men);
And some of them were drunkards,
    It cannot be denied;
But one washed all their sins away
    When Sidney Carton died.

The gentlemen of Dickens
  Are round us here to-day,
For their self-sacrificing
  Brave spirits live for aye.
They cheer my heart and lift it,
  They set my blood aglow,
For I was once a gentleman,
  Though it was years ago.

Do They Think That I Do Not Know?

They say that I never have written of love,
  As a writer of songs should do;
They say that I never could touch the strings
  With a touch that is firm and true;
They say I know nothing of women and men
  In the fields where Love's roses grow,
And they say I must write with a halting pen—
  Do you think that I do not know?

When the love-burst came, like an English Spring,
  In the days when our hair was brown,
And the hem of her skirt was a sacred thing

76

And her hair was an angel's crown;
The shock when another man touched her arm,
    Where the dancers sat round in a row;
The hope and despair, and the false alarm—
    Do you think that I do not know?

By the arbour lights on the western farms,
    You remember the question put,
While you held her warm in your quivering arms
    And you trembled from head to foot;
The electric shock from her finger tips,
    And the murmuring answer low,
The soft, shy yielding of warm red lips—
    Do you think that I do not know?

She was buried at Brighton, where Gordon sleeps,
    When I was a world away;
And the sad old garden its secret keeps,
    For nobody knows to-day.
She left a message for me to read,
    Where the wild wide oceans flow;
Do you know how the heart of a man can bleed—
    Do you think that I do not know?

I stood by the grave where the dead girl lies,
    When the sunlit scenes were fair,
And the white clouds high in the autumn skies,
    And I answered the message there.
But the haunting words of the dead to me
    Shall go wherever I go.
She lives in the Marriage that Might Have Been—
    Do you think that I do not know?

They sneer or scoff, and they pray or groan,
    And the false friend plays his part.
Do you think that the blackguard who drinks alone
    Knows aught of a pure girl's heart?
Knows aught of the first pure love of a boy
    With his warm young blood aglow,
Knows aught of the thrill of the world-old joy—
    Do you think that I do not know?

They say that I never have written of love,
    They say that my heart is such
That finer feelings are far above;
    But a writer may know too much.
There are darkest depths in the brightest nights,
    When the clustering stars hang low;
There are things it would break his strong heart to write—
    Do you think that I do not know?

[*1910*]

The Route March

Did you hear the children singing, O my brothers?
Did you hear the children singing as our troops went
marching past?
In the sunshine and the rain
As they'll never sing again—
Hear the little school-girls singing as our troops went
swinging past?

Did you hear the children singing, O my brothers?
Did you hear the children singing for the first man and the last?
As they marched away and vanished,
To a tune we thought was banished—
Did you hear the children singing for the future and the past?

Shall you hear the children singing, O my brothers?
Shall you hear the children singing in the sunshine or the rain?
There'll be sobs beneath the ringing
Of the cheers, and 'neath the singing
There'll be tears of orphan children when Our Boys come
back again!

[1915—July?]

On the Night Train

Have you seen the bush by moonlight, from the train, go
running by?
Blackened log and stump and sapling, ghostly trees all dead
and dry;
Here a patch of glassy water; there a glimpse of mystic sky?
Have you heard the still voice calling—yet so warm, and yet
so cold:
"I'm the Mother-Bush that bore you! Come to me when you
are old"?

Did you see the Bush below you sweeping darkly to the Range,
All unchanged and all unchanging, yet so *very* old and strange!
While you thought in softened anger of the things that did
estrange?
(Did you hear the Bush a-calling, when your heart was young
and bold:
"I'm the Mother-Bush that nursed you; come to me when you
are old"?)

In the cutting, in the tunnel, out of sight of stack or shed,
Have you heard the grey Bush calling from the pine-ridge
overhead:
"You have seen the seas and cities; all is cold to you, or dead—
All seems done and all seems told—
But the grey-light turns to gold!
I'm the Mother-Bush that loves you; come to me now you are old"?

[*Sydney, 19th February 1922*]

Index of Titles

Andy's Gone With Cattle   *10*
Andy's Return   *11*
The Army of the Rear   *3*
The Ballad of the Drover   *14*
The Blue Mountains   *13*
The City Bushman   *36*
Dan Wasn't Thrown from his Horse   *30*
Do They Think That I Do Not Know?   *76*
Faces in the Street   *6*
Freedom on the Wallaby   *31*
The Gentlemen of Dickens   *74*
The Ghost   *17*
The Glass on the Bar   *26*
Golden Gully   *1*
The Grog-an'-Grumble Steeplechase   *40*
The Horseman on the Skyline   *71*
I'll Tell You What, You Wanderers   *50*
The King and Queen and I   *70*
Lake Eliza   *46*
The Men Who Come Behind   *53*
Middleton's Rouseabout   *24*
The Morning of New Zealand   *45*
My Father-in-law and I   *73*
The Old Bark School   *56*
The Old Jimmy Woodser   *58*
On the Night Train   *80*
Out Back   *47*
The Pavement Stones: A Song of the Unemployed   *27*
Reedy River   *51*
The Roaring Days   *20*
The Route March   *79*

The Rush to London   *63*
Second Class Wait Here   *60*
The Separation   *66*
The Shearers   *64*
The Sliprails and the Spur   *61*
The Statue of our Queen   *29*
The Teams   *23*
To Hannah   *67*
To Jim   *68*
The Uncultured Rhymer to his Cultured Critics   *55*
Up the Country   *33*
The Watch on the Kerb   *5*
When the Irish Flag Went By   *32*
When Your Pants Begin To Go   *43*

Index of First Lines

A cloud of dust on the long white road   **23**
Above the ashes straight and tall   **13**
Across the stony ridges   **14**
Did you hear the children singing, O my brothers?   **79**
Down the street as I was drifting with the city's human tide   **17**
Fight through ignorance, want, and care —   **55**
Have you seen the bush by moonlight, from the train, go running by?   **80**
I am back from up the country — very sorry that I went —   **33**
I gaze upon my son once more   **68**
I listened through the music and the sounds of revelry   **3**
I'll tell you what, you wanderers, who drift from town to town   **50**
In the morning of New Zealand we should sing a Marseillaise!   **45**
It was pleasant up the country, City Bushman, where you went   **36**
It was built of bark and poles, and the floor was full of holes   **56**
My father-in-law is a careworn man   **73**
Night-lights are falling   **5**
No church-bell rings them from the Track   **64**
No one lives in Golden Gully, for its golden days are o'er   **1**
O Scotty, have you visited the Picture Gallery   **70**
On suburban railway stations — you may see them as you pass —   **60**
Our Andy's gone to battle now   **10**

Our fathers toiled for bitter bread   *31*
Pride, selfishness in every line   *29*
Spirit girl to whom 'twas given   *67*
Tall and freckled and sandy   *24*
Ten miles down Reedy River   *51*
The colours of the setting sun   *61*
The gentlemen of Dickens   *74*
The night too quickly passes   *20*
The old Jimmy Woodser comes into the bar   *58*
The old year went, and the new returned, in the withering
    weeks of drought   *47*
The sand was heavy on our feet   *46*
There's a class of men (and women) who are always on their
    guard —   *53*
They lie, the men who tell us for reasons of their own   *6*
They say he was thrown and run over   *30*
They say that I never have written of love   *76*
Three bushmen one morning rode up to an inn   *26*
'Twas Eight-Hour Day, and proudly   *32*
'Twixt the coastline and the border lay the town of Grog-an'-
    Grumble   *40*
We knew too little of the world   *66*
When first I came to town, resolved   *27*
When you wear a cloudy collar and a shirt that isn't
    white   *43*
Who's that mysterious rider   *71*
With pannikins all rusty   *11*
You're off away to London now   *63*